Two zebras

Daubenton's bat

Wings are folded up

Young explorer playing with pouncing cat

Loose quills can stick in an attacker's skin

Cow feeding on hay

Porcupine

EXPLORERS

Mammals

Written by
DAVID BURNIE

DORLING KINDERSLEY, INC.

NEW YORK

A DORLING KINDERSLEY BOOK

Senior editor Susan McKeever **Art editor** Vicky Wharton
Assistant editor Djinn von Noorden **U.S. Editor** Charles A. Wills
Production Catherine Semark **Editorial consultant** Henry Schofield
Photography by Jane Burton, Dave King, Kim Taylor
First American Edition, 1993
2 4 6 8 10 9 7 5 3 1
Published in the United States by
Dorling Kindersley, Inc., 232 Madison Avenue
New York, New York 10016

ISBN 1-56458-228-0

Library of Congress Catalog Card Number 92-54312

Color reproduction by Colourscan, Singapore
Printed in Italy by A. Mondadori Editore, Verona

Contents

8. Looking at mammals

10. What is a mammal?

12. Mammals everywhere

14. On the alert

16. Furry friends

18. Mammals on the move

20. Clues on the ground

22. Mammals that fly

24. How mammals feed

26. Keeping clean

28. Defending a territory

30. The newborn mammal

32. Life in a pouch

34. Careful parents

36. Playing

38. Hunting mammals

40. Life in a group

42. Hiding away

44. Special defense

46. Hibernating and storing food

48. Field and forest mammals

50. Mountain mammals

52. Desert mammals

54. Freshwater mammals

56. Mammals of the sea

58. City mammals

60. Index

Looking at mammals

Mammals live almost anywhere you can think of. Squirrels run around the treetops, mice scurry through the undergrowth, raccoons feed in parks, and bats fly through the air. But mammals are alert animals. If they sense that you are nearby, they will quickly run for cover. To watch mammals, you need to learn how to move quietly, without giving yourself away.

Spotting mammals
What has fur or hair, four limbs, and feeds its young on milk? The answer is a squirrel – or any other mammal that lives on land.

The squirrel's big eyes and ears show that it has keen senses, like other mammals.

The squirrel uses its front paws like hands to hold its food and to groom itself.

The squirrel has a thick coat of fur. It also has long whiskers that help it feel its way.

Moving upwind

Many mammals use their keen sense of smell to detect people and other animals. You can make sure a mammal cannot smell you by moving into the wind toward it. The wind will blow your scent away so the animal cannot smell it.

These notes record what a squirrel looks like, where it was seen, and what it was eating.

To find out which way the wind is blowing, throw some grass or leaves into the air and see which way they move.

Nature notebook

Try drawing the mammals that you see. Record what kind of habitat they live in, how they move, and what they eat. You don't have to be a gifted artist to make a useful notebook – even a quick sketch with notes will help you remember details.

Mammal watching

Wear dull-colored clothes when mammal-watching. Binoculars are very useful for watching shy mammals such as deer. If you use them, remember to keep down so that the animals cannot see your shape against the sky.

Many mammals come out to feed at dusk, so this is a good time to use your binoculars.

What is a mammal?

You may know that you are related to monkeys. But did you know that you are also related to bats, tigers, whales, kangaroos, and many more creatures? We are all mammals, linked together by several features. Mammals all have hair or fur, most give birth to live young (instead of laying eggs), and all feed their young on milk.

Largest on land

Elephants are the largest mammals that live on land. There are two types of elephant – African and Indian. Check the type by the ear rule – African elephants have big, floppy ears, while Indian elephants' ears are smaller.

This African elephant has extra large ears to keep it cool in the heat.

An elephant's trunk works like a nose, a hand, and even a shower.

Thick skin with little hair

Thick legs hold up the elephant's heavy body.

All mammals, from elephants to mice, are warm-blooded. They can live in hot or cold places.

Dolphins only have hair around the mouth – they make up for no hair elsewhere by thick layers of fat.

Swimming mammal

A dolphin may look like a fish, but it is really a special kind of mammal. The biggest animal in the world – the blue whale – is another mammal that spends the whole of its life in water.

Lots in common

Humans and dogs look quite different, but both are mammals and have bodies that are built on the same plan. Like most mammals, dogs move on four legs. After we learn to walk, we move on two.

The echidna has a coat of spines, like a hedgehog.

Tall story

Giraffes are the tallest mammals. At 20 feet, they're taller than any kind of animal. With their long necks, they stretch high into trees to feed on leaves that other animals cannot reach.

Ant-eating egg layer

This spiny mammal is called an echidna (*ek-id-nah*). It is one of the few mammals that lays eggs instead of giving birth to live young. The leathery egg sticks to a patch of skin on the mother's body until it hatches. Echidnas like to feast on ants.

11

Mammals everywhere

Long ago, all mammals lived in the wild. There were no such things as pet dogs and cats or farm animals. But gradually, people discovered how to keep mammals and make them tame. Now you can make friends with mammals everywhere – at home, on the farm, in the zoo, and at the riding stables.

Pet gerbil
In the wild, gerbils live in dry places and feed on plants and seeds. They make good pets because they are very tame and live happily in a cage.

The horse
Before railroads and cars were invented, the fastest way to get from one place to another was by horse. Horses were kept everywhere, including towns and cities. Today, the place to see horses is in fields or riding stables.

Before you can ride a horse, it has to be trained.

Horses and ponies that people ride have long, slender legs.

Why do horses wear metal shoes? To stop their hooves from wearing away on hard roads.

On safari

A car makes a good lookout post for seeing how mammals live.
Mammals are suspicious of people, but they will often ignore a
car – as long as you remember to stay inside!

*A cat's good eyesight
and hearing make it
an expert hunter.*

*Healthy domestic
cat with thick,
shiny fur.*

Independent pets

For thousands of years, people
have kept cats as pets. But cats
still have a wild side to their
nature. They are born hunters. Even if
a cat is well fed, it cannot help trying to
track down and catch small animals.
You probably know this already if you
have a pet cat!

*Holstein cows are bred
specially for their milk.*

Furry farm friends

Farmers breed farm mammals in a special way
to make them useful to us.
Cows produce much
more milk than
their wild
relatives. Pigs
are bigger,
and sheep
grow more
wool.

On the alert

Have you ever wondered what the world seems like to the animals around you? Try looking at the way different mammals use their senses. We find out about the world mainly by using our eyes. For other mammals, smell and hearing are more important.

On the trail
When a bloodhound takes a sniff, air travels through special spaces inside the front of its head. Here, millions of nerve endings react to different substances in the air. Together, the substances make up a scent that the bloodhound remembers.

This dog can detect smells a million times better than a human can.

Bloodhounds have good hearing but cannot see as well as we can.

The fennec fox's large ears work like radiators. They give off heat and keep its body cool.

Early warning

With its giant ears and large eyes, a hare is quick to notice anything that might spell trouble. It can see all around without moving its head.

Night patrol

As night falls over the desert, the tiny fennec fox sets off to look for food. With its keen eyes, it can see on even the darkest night. A sensitive nose and huge ears also help it to hunt in the darkness.

Which way did it go?

If you take a dog for a walk, watch what happens when it crosses a scent. It will often move one way and then the other, figuring out which direction the animal or person went.

Long, stiff whiskers

Wonder whisker

A rat can move around in complete darkness, using its whiskers to feel the way. Its whiskers are thicker and stiffer than normal hairs. If they touch anything, the rat feels them move.

Furry friends

Most mammals have a furry coat – even you! Hair, or fur, helps mammals keep their bodies at just the right temperature – not too hot or too cold. Hair traps a layer of air near the body; this helps stop heat from escaping to the world outside.

Humans don't have as much hair as most mammals. We have to wear clothes to keep warm.

Well wrapped up

Sheep have a thick, soft kind of hair called wool. The strands of wool are all tangled together. When a sheep's wool is shorn (cut off), it comes away in a large lump called a fleece.

Lanolin makes wool feel greasy.

A sheep's wool grows all year round. If it is not shorn, it can get very long.

Natural wool is coated with an oily substance called lanolin. This helps stop the wool from soaking up water when it rains.

Cooling down

Next time you see a racehorse after a race, notice how its coat steams from sweating so much. It cannot take off its clothes when it gets too hot, like we can. Instead it keeps cool by sweating. When the sweat dries, it uses up some of the body's heat.

During a race, a horse gets very hot. It cools down by making lots of sweat.

Goose pimples

Have you ever wondered why your skin turns bumpy when you are cold or frightened? It happens because tiny muscles make your hair stand on end. Long ago, when humans had much more hair, this would have kept us warm or made us look bigger to enemies.

The easiest places to see goose bumps are on your arms and legs. Each bump is at the base of a hair.

A panting dog sticks out its tongue and breathes quickly. Air flows around its tongue and mouth and cools it down.

Hot pants

We pant when we are out of breath. Dogs also pant, but not always for the same reason. A dog cannot sweat. If it is hot, it uses panting to help it cool down. See how many panting dogs you can spot on the next really hot day.

Mammals on the move

What do we have in common with kangaroos? One answer is that, like kangaroos, we can get around on two legs. In the world of mammals, moving on two legs is not very common. Most mammals move on all fours, and their legs and feet have become specially shaped to fit the way in which they live.

A natural acrobat

For a squirrel, tree branches are like paths in the air. Its sharp claws grip the bark as it scampers along high above the ground. Good eyesight helps it judge distances when it leaps from one tree to another.

If a squirrel spots you, it will climb out of sight to the opposite side of a tree trunk.

The squirrel's legs are short but powerful.

Bushy tail helps squirrel to balance along thin branches

Body is crouched and ready for take-off

Legs unfold and push the kangaroo's body into the air

Heavy tail swings out for balance

Legs come forward to touch the ground, ready for another jump

Front legs are tucked close to body

On the hop

When kangaroos need to get around quickly, they hold their small front legs in the air and bound forward on their back legs alone. But when they feed, they often hop slowly forward on all fours.

Some monkeys can hang on with their tails.

Feet or hands?

Long toes mean that monkeys and apes can grip branches with their feet. This helps them to climb trees.

Changing speed

A horse has four ways of moving – walking, trotting, cantering, or galloping. When it walks, it keeps its legs almost straight. When it gallops, its legs bend and then straighten out.

Slender legs are powered by big muscles packed close to the body.

19

Clues on the ground

Mouse and rat tracks are small, with long claw marks.

Looking for mammals in the wild is not easy. For mammals are always on the alert for danger. The slightest sound will send them rushing into hiding. But look down – if the ground is damp, you may see clues that prove wild mammals were around only minutes before you arrived!

Cushion feet

A camel has feet that are perfectly made for desert life. Cushiony foot pads spread the camel's weight evenly over the sand, and stop it from sinking.

This dog is on tiptoes – this is the end of its foot.

The faster the animal is moving, the greater the gap between the groups of tracks.

Paws and claws

Dogs and cats walk on their toes. You can tell a cat print from a dog print by the claw marks. Dogs can't pull their claws in, so they are always visible. But cats keep their claws stowed away until they are needed for scratching.

Dogs' claws are visible in the paw print.

Dogs have a little toe pad and a bigger pad on each of their paws.

Single hoof

Horses have hooves with just one toe. The toe is covered with hard horn, like your big toenail. Horse prints are easy to recognize – they are in just one piece. Some of the prints you see will be from domestic horses with shoes.

Horses and deer walk on their tiptoes, just like dogs and cats.

Shoeless horse print

Metal shoes protect horses' hooves and stop them from wearing down or splitting.

Cloven hoof

Like horses, deer have hooves. But their prints look different because their hooves are made from two toes. These types of hooves are called cloven (divided) hooves.

Reindeer hooves are spread out to support them in the snow.

Making tracks

Why not take a track home with you? Look for tracks near muddy stream banks, by fences, or on damp ground or sand. Find a good clear print, and remove any leaves or soil around it. You'll need a strong cardboard ring secured with a paper-clip, a mixing bowl and spoon, some plaster of Paris, and water.

Place cardboard ring around print

Mix plaster of Paris with water until runny

Pour paste into ring and smooth over surface

Lift up cast when dry to see your print

Mammals that fly

Many people are afraid of bats. They do not like the way that they flutter around after dark. But bats are fascinating and harmless animals. They are the only mammals that can fly, and they are much more interested in finding food than in bothering humans. Some bats live on fruit and flowers. Others hunt insects.

Where bats live
Bats spend the day asleep in buildings, caves, or holes in trees. As night falls, they set off to hunt.

A bat's wing is a flap of skin stretched between bony "fingers." The thumb forms a short hook.

Big ear
It's not hard to see how the long-eared bat gets its name. It uses its giant ears to detect faint echoes from flying insects. Each ear is made of two separate flaps. This bat goes for a big sleep in the winter and tucks the large ear flaps under its wings.

Insect-eating bats have tiny eyes and cannot see well. Their teeth are small but sharp.

Hunting by sound

A bat hunts by making high-pitched sounds which we cannot hear. The sounds bounce off flying insects, and the bat homes in on the echo to catch its prey.

Echoes tell a bat where an insect is and how far away it is.

Claws cling tightly to catkin

Life upside-down

When bats are not in the air, they spend most of their time upside-down. Their back feet have sharp claws, and they use these to grip rough surfaces. Baby bats cannot fly, so they have to be careful to hold on tight.

This is an adult Daubenton's bat. You can see it flying over rivers and streams, catching insects.

Wings folded up

Make sure you go out at dusk, or the bats will not be around yet.

Attract a bat

If you find a place where bats often fly, see what happens if you gently throw a small piece of bread into the air. The bats will swoop down to investigate.

🖐 *Never throw stones at bats.*

23

How mammals feed

Next time you eat a meal, see if it contains food that has come from animals as well as food that comes from plants. You are an omnivore, meaning that you can eat food of all kinds. But many more mammals eat just plants or meat and not both. The plant-eaters are called herbivores, while meat-eaters are called carnivores.

Chewing twice
Grass and hay are difficult to digest. In order to digest them properly, a cow has to chew twice. First it chews the grass into a pulp and swallows it. Then it chews the pulp a second time so that its digestion can be completed.

Grass is not a very rich food, so cows have to eat a lot of it every day to stay alive. During the winter months, farmers feed their cows with hay (dried grass).

A lion uses the sharp teeth on the sides of its jaws to crack bones.

Living on meat

Lions live mostly on meat. Their strong jaws open very wide – a lion can crack a large bone with just one bite. They usually hunt large animals, but will eat lizards, tortoises, or even insects.

Plant-eaters have sharp teeth for cutting, but also flat teeth for chewing and grinding.

Meat-eaters have teeth with sharp edges that can slice through meat.

Chopping and chewing

When you eat a sandwich, you bite off a mouthful at a time and then chew it up. Chewing makes the food ready for your stomach.

Looking at leftovers

Mammals that eat nuts and other seeds each have their own way of getting at their food. Look for the remains of nuts and seeds in parks and woods and along hedges. You might be able to figure out which animals have been feeding on them.

A bank vole makes a rough hole without teeth marks.

A wood mouse chews the hard scales off a pine cone.

A wood mouse leaves small teeth marks on the edge of the hole.

25

Keeping clean

Wild mammals don't spend any time in the bathroom, but they are just as careful as we are about keeping clean. Instead of washing with soap and water, mammals with thick fur "groom" themselves with their claws and teeth. Mammals without much fur, such as hippos and elephants, take mud or dust baths.

Time for a wash

We groom ourselves by washing our hair and skin. Soap and shampoo are designed not to harm the skin. Stronger detergents, such as washing powder, can take away the natural oils that keep the skin healthy.

Glorious mud

Wallowing in mud looks like a way to get dirty rather than a way of staying healthy. But a hippo's skin is sensitive and has to be protected from the hot sun. Mud and a special skin oil help screen the sun's rays.

Taking turns

Fur is a perfect hiding place for small blood-sucking animals such as ticks and fleas. These can be difficult for animals to pick off, so sometimes one helps another with the task. Chimpanzees spend many hours relaxing together by grooming each other's fur in this way.

When fur gets wet it sticks together, and won't keep the animal warm.

Caught in the rain

Watch carefully the next time you see a dog or a cat come in from the rain. A dog shakes itself, but a cat carefully licks raindrops from its fur.

A good licking

A cat keeps its fur spotless by washing and combing it with its tongue and teeth. To clean hard-to-reach places like its face, the cat licks a front paw and then wipes the paw over its fur.

The cat uses its teeth to straighten out any tangles in its fur.

The cat wets its fur with its tongue and then swallows any dirt that is caught on it.

A cat's tongue is covered with spines that work like a comb.

27

Defending a territory

For wild mammals, life is like a competition. The winners are the animals that manage to find the most food and that have the most young. To give themselves the best chances of getting ahead, male mammals often claim a piece of ground called a territory. They defend their territory by fighting with their rivals.

Necks in a twist
Giraffes have one of the strangest ways of fighting of all mammals. Instead of biting, kicking, or battling with their horns, they push against each other, neck to neck.

Test of strength
When rams fight, they run at each other and push their heads together as hard as they can. The loser is the animal that gets pushed backward. The big curly horns of these bighorn rams stay out of the fight, so the animals rarely get hurt.

Horns are made of the same hard substance that we have in our hair, fingernails, and toenails.

Red deer grow a new set of antlers each year. After the breeding season, the antlers fall off.

Head-on clash

During the breeding season, called the rut, male red deer battle head-on for the possession of females. They lock their antlers together. The fight may look dangerous, but the deer are hardly ever hurt. The battle ends when the loser runs away.

Spotting signs

If you look carefully at young trees in a wood, you may be able to see where deer have rubbed their scent on to the bark. Look out, too, for places where deer have eaten the bark.

Bark where deer have rubbed their scent looks frayed.

Smelly signpost

Many mammals use scent to show where their territories start and finish. Deer have special scent glands near their eyes. By rubbing its face against a tree, a deer leaves a "signpost" that other deer will smell.

Floating fighters

A bull hippo weighs more than a car. When it fights with a rival, it uses its long front teeth as weapons. Fights between hippos are long and fierce, and sometimes the loser dies.

The newborn mammal

For humans, raising young is a slow business. It takes nine months for you to develop inside your mother's body and many years for you to become an adult. But for small mammals, life is much faster. A mother rat can have up to 11 young at one time, and she can have a whole new family every four weeks!

Mouse house
Many small mammals bring up their young in special nests. See if you can spot a harvest mouse nest in a field or a hedge – it is about the size of a tennis ball.

See how we grow
Like all mammals, humans change shape as they grow up. When you are born, your head looks very big compared to the rest of you. But as you get older, the rest of your body grows much more quickly.

Mini adult
Only a few hours old, but already a mini version of an adult, this guinea pig has spent about two months growing inside its mother's body. It sucks on mother's milk for three weeks, but in just a day, it will begin to nibble solid food as well.

Furry coat

Head looks big compared to rest of body.

Helpless infant

A newborn rat is completely helpless. It comes into the world after only 21 days in its mother's body. Blind and hairless, it hardly looks like a mammal at all. It feeds on its mother's milk for three weeks.

Rat has grown a thick coat of fur

Restless rat

A three-week-old rat is almost ready to start life on its own. It may still drink some of its mother's milk, but it spends more and more of its time searching for different food.

The head looks smaller in relation to the body now.

Bigger and bolder

This three-week-old guinea pig looks the same as the newborn one, only bigger! At this stage, it is able to look after itself. Within another six weeks, it will be ready to have young of its own.

Guinea pig is nearly full grown.

Life in a pouch

Imagine being carried around in a warm pouch on your mother's belly. This is what happens to marsupials (*mar-soo-pee-als*), mammals with a difference. They are born when they are still tiny, and they do most of their growing up inside their mother's special pouch. The pouch keeps the young warm and safe, and it also contains teats that produce milk.

Mobile home

This female red-necked wallaby keeps its young in its pouch for about four months. After that, the young wallaby, or "joey" starts to venture outside.

You'll see marsupials in Australia, and also in North and South America.

The pouch is like a big, stretchy bag that is open at the top.

Strong tail for balance when leaping

Hanging on

The Virginia opossum is a marsupial from North America. The mother's pouch is more like a flap than a bag, and it does not cover her young. The Virginia opossum can have 40 or 50 young, but she has only 13 teats. Only the young that find a teat to suck on survive.

Older opossums cling to their mother's fur.

Joey's first journey

You could hold a newborn joey in your hand – it's barely bigger than a jellybean! When a joey is born, only its front legs work. It clambers through its mother's fur, and then it drops into her pouch.

Jump aboard!

As it grows up, the joey spends more and more of its time outside its mother's pouch. But if danger threatens, it jumps back aboard.

The joey puts its front legs into the pouch. The mother lets the pouch go loose.

The joey turns as it jumps aboard.

The joey's tail lies over its head.

A grown joey cannot fit inside the pouch. Its head, back legs, and tail stick out.

33

Careful parents

Mammals take extra-special care of their young. They feed them with milk, teach them how to behave, and guard them from danger. Being a careful parent is hard work. A mother cat is on duty for several weeks, but some mammals, such as humans or elephants, look after their young for many years.

Mother on duty
This mother pig looks sleepy and contented. But if anything threatens her piglets, she will quickly rush to protect them. Her powerful jaws can give a nasty bite.

Have you ever seen this sight in a farmyard? Notice how each piglet always sucks from the same teat.

A mother pig produces milk from two lines of teats underneath her body. The piglets push and shove as they struggle to find a teat.

Babe in arms

Humans, chimpanzees, and gorillas hold their young in the same way – by cradling them in their arms. Unlike kittens, we don't have lots of loose skin. For us, being picked up by the scruff of the neck would be uncomfortable and also dangerous.

A gorilla supports its baby in its arms, while the baby clings to its fur.

What a mouthful!

A mother cat cannot pick up her kittens with her paws. Instead, she carries them in her mouth.

Her kittens know to keep quiet and still.

Sow (female pig) listens out for danger to her piglets with her big ears.

Follow the leader

Very young mammals stay close to their parents. Baby hedgehogs follow their mother in a line. If one of them gets lost, it makes a whistling sound to call for its mother's help.

Auntie elephant

A young elephant is looked after not only by its own mother, but by another female, called an "aunt." The aunt gives the young elephant extra protection.

Playing

If you have ever had a puppy or a kitten, you will know that they spend a lot of their time playing. When young animals play, they get exercise, and they practice skills that they will need in adult life. These skills include moving quickly and easily, dealing with food, and keeping in touch with other members of their species.

Gibbons have very long arms, making them great swingers.

Who's in charge?

Mammals that live in groups, such as dogs, often have a chain of command, with one animal at the top. Playing puppies try out different expressions to show where they fit into the group. A snarling face means "I'm in charge."

By playing, the young gibbon finds out which kind of branches will bear its weight.

Only playing

Playing is just as important for humans as for other mammals. It builds up our muscles and helps us learn different ways of using our hands. Playing also helps us communicate with each other, both with our voices and with our faces.

The gibbon has to judge exactly how far to swing as it moves around among the branches.

Playing builds up the gibbon's muscles.

Getting the hang of it

An adult gibbon knows the best way to climb trees, and it is very good at judging the distance between one branch and another. A young gibbon has to learn this by playing.

A gibbon can hang on with its feet as well as its arms. Its big toes work like thumbs to help it hold on.

Fake fight

Fox cubs and other young animals "play-fight." When they do this, they learn how to pin each other down and how to use their teeth. This trains them for hunting and also for dealing with rival foxes. Although this fight looks serious, neither of the cubs will be harmed.

Next time you see some young animals play-fighting, notice how carefully they use their teeth. They bite each other very gently.

A cub shows defeat by lying on its back and pointing its ears backward.

37

Hunting mammals

Lions, tigers, wolves, bats, and shrews are just some of the many mammals that hunt other animals for food. Some hunting mammals work on their own. Others, such as lions and wolves, hunt in groups and work close together to make sure that their prey cannot escape. All hunting mammals have sharp senses and are quick to spot the chance of a meal.

A zebra can run faster than a lion, but a lion can catch it by creeping up on it quietly.

Shrews find their food mainly by smell and by using their whiskers.

Tiny hunter
Smaller than a mouse, the pygmy shrew feeds on earthworms and other small animals. To stay alive, it has to eat nearly its own weight in food every day.

Pouncing lion

Male lions are big and powerful, but they are not very good at hunting. Most of the work is done by the females. They hunt in small groups, creeping low over the ground toward their prey. When they are close enough, they suddenly pounce.

Testing a hunter

What makes a cat pounce? Is it sound? Or is it the sight of an animal or the way that it moves? Find out for yourself by making a paper mouse and seeing how a cat reacts.

2 See if the cat is interested when the mouse is still. Now see what happens if you pull the string smoothly, and then in short jerks. What does the cat do if you try again in the dark?

1 Make a "mouse" by rolling up some paper and fastening it with tape. Attach a piece of string to one end.

Within a few minutes this earthworm will be chewed up and swallowed.

Life in a group

Some mammals lead a solitary life, but others live in a group. This is not just for the company! Group members look after one another, and one stands guard while others feed or sleep safely. Groups may consist of some males, females, and their young. Young males are often pushed out of the group. Then they may form a "bachelor" group.

Thump alarm
A thumping sound and a flash of white spells danger to rabbits. A frightened rabbit thumps on the ground with its hind feet to alert its companions. Then it raises its white fluffy tail and leaps to safety into the nearest burrow.

Life in the warren
On the surface, a rabbit home looks like just a lot of holes in the grass. But underneath the ground is a bustling network of burrows called a warren. Does (female rabbits) have about ten babies each year. After four months, the young are able to breed themselves. So numbers grow quickly in the warren.

The doe covers the stop with earth when she's not there.

Breeding burrow is called a stop

Safety in numbers

Zebras in a group present a confusing striped mixture to predators – especially at night. Some stand head to tail and groom each other, or swat flies off each other's faces with their tails.

One zebra is always on the lookout for danger while the others feed and sleep.

Female family

Elephants live in family groups of females and their young. The eldest female, called the matriarch, leads the group. It's tough on the males when they grow up – they are pushed out of the group and have to live alone.

The grass around warrens is usually cropped short by munching rabbits.

Rabbits make their burrows by digging with their forepaws.

Rabbits usually feed at night. They spend much of the day resting underground.

41

Hiding away

Imagine you are in a forest in Northern India. The forest floor is very dim, except where shafts of sunlight shine through gaps in the leaves. Suddenly, a movement catches your eye – a tiger is on the move. You didn't see it because it was camouflaged – blended perfectly into the background. The tiger is only one of many mammals that hide away in order to survive or hunt without being noticed.

Stripe secret
The tiger's black and orange stripes match the pattern made by the sun on the grass and trees. This keeps the tiger hidden until it is close enough to its prey to pounce.

Light brown fur matches dead leaves

Big cat
The tiger is the biggest cat of all, so it's amazing that it can hide away so well. Young tiger cubs are born with light-colored stripes which darken to the vivid black and orange after a few months.

Tigers from cold places have much lighter fur. It hides them against snow.

The leveret lies flat and holds its long ears close to its body.

Hiding in the grass

A leveret (baby hare) grows up in a hollow in the ground called a form. When its mother goes away to feed, the leveret lies down in the form and keeps very still. This hides it from hunting animals.

Living camouflage

Sloths spend their whole lives hanging from tree branches. Their fur has a green color because it is full of tiny, living plants. The plants help the sloth to hide.

Black stripes help to break up the tiger's outline.

Hidden in the forest

A newborn deer, called a fawn, cannot run away from danger. Instead, it lies very still on the forest floor. Fawns often have spotted fur. The spots help to break up the outlines of a fawn's body, in the same way that stripes hide a tiger.

Many deer have spotted fur only when they are young.

The spots look like patches of sunlight on the forest floor.

Special defense

For wild mammals, life is full of danger. Every time they set off in search of food, they run the risk of being discovered and eaten. But many small mammals have special ways of defending themselves. If they are cornered by something larger and more powerful, these defenses give them a chance of survival.

The cat's tail seems to swell up as its fur stands on end.

Puss in danger

Have you ever seen a cat all puffed up and angry like this? This is a cat's way of defending itself. When danger threatens, a cat can change itself from something soft and sleek into something that looks and sounds very dangerous. With luck, its enemy will leave it alone.

With its back arched, the cat is ready to spring forward at its enemy.

The cat hisses and bares its teeth – showing that it is ready for a fight.

44

A stink in the tail

If a skunk is attacked, it sprays a horrible-smelling liquid at its enemy. While the attacker coughs and chokes, the skunk makes its getaway.

Sudden death

The possum has a special way of getting out of trouble – it pretends to be dead. It lets its body go limp and its tongue hang out. Faced with this, an attacker soon loses interest!

Spiky surprise

Would you believe that this spiky thing is a mammal? A porcupine has special hairs called quills that are hard and very sharp. If threatened, it turns its back to its attacker and rattles its quills. If this doesn't frighten the enemy off, the porcupine backs into it. Ouch!

A porcupine's quills are very loosely attached. They can get stuck in an attacker's skin and cause nasty wounds.

Back to front

As long as a porcupine keeps its back to an enemy (usually a lion or a leopard), it can fend off an attack.

45

Hibernating and storing food

Winter is a difficult time for small mammals. When the weather gets cold, food becomes hard to find. Some mammals solve this problem by hibernating. They fall asleep and only wake up properly when winter is over. Other mammals stay awake and survive by eating food that they have hidden away during summer and autumn.

When a dormouse hibernates, its heart beats very slowly and its whole body slows down.

Sleeping the winter away
In countries where the winters are cold, a dormouse may spend more than half the year asleep. Before it starts to hibernate, the dormouse eats as much as it can and gets very fat. This fat keeps it alive through the winter.

The dormouse makes its winter nest from bark, grass, leaves, and moss. It curls up inside with its tail over its face.

Food in the bank

Take a quick peek into old tree holes when you next go for a forest walk – you might find a squirrel store! Like hamsters, squirrels store food for the winter. They collect seeds and nuts and hide them away in holes either in trees or in the ground.

Built-in bags

If you or your friends have a pet hamster, you know that hamsters have a special way of carrying food. In the wild, hamsters live in places where it is often cold in winter. They stuff food into special cheek pouches and carry it into their burrows to use as a winter supply.

When a hamster finds some food, it picks it up with its front feet and begins to eat.

The hamster doesn't stop when it is full, Instead, it stores the leftover food in its cheek pouches.

With its cheeks bulging like balloons, the hamster is ready to take the spare food back to its burrow.

Time to wake up!

Hibernation is not like ordinary sleep. A hibernating dormouse will sleep through almost anything – including being picked up! But when winter comes to an end, the dormouse's built-in "alarm clock" gradually wakes it up.

Field and forest mammals

Mammals like living in fields and forests. There is plenty for them to eat and there are lots of hiding places where they can bring up their young. Many field and forest mammals are shy and will either "freeze" or run away if they hear you. To see them, the best plan is to sit and wait. Listen carefully for any sounds the animals make as they move around.

Is it a bear?

The koala lives only in forests in eastern Australia, where it feeds on the leaves of gum trees. Although people call it the koala "bear," it isn't really a bear at all, but a marsupial – a mammal with a pouch.

Danger above

Tucked away in their burrow, a family of wood mice are safe from most of their enemies. But if a weasel smells them, their burrow can become a deadly trap. The mice cannot escape, and the weasel is slender and flexible enough to slip inside and eat them.

Look out for slim, sleek weasels sniffing at burrow entrances.

Wood mice go out to feed at night.

48

Fur detective

In fields and woodlands, look closely at any rough bark or barbed wire. You will often find strands of hair, left behind by different types of mammals brushing past.

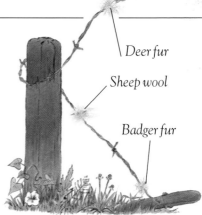

Deer fur

Sheep wool

Badger fur

Sheep wool looks dense and feels oily.

What is it from?

If you look at animal hair under a magnifying glass, you can find out what it came from. Rabbit hairs are gray and soft. Deer, fox, and badger hairs are longer and thicker.

Vole in the grass

You may find bank voles, small mouselike mammals, difficult to spot. They stay out of sight to protect themselves from predators. Voles scurry along covered pathways through grass and leaves. When winter comes, they move around beneath the snow.

Voles have more rounded noses than those of mice.

Voles have longer, shaggier hair than that of mice.

Mountain mammals

High up in mountains, the air cannot hold much heat, so high mountains are usually cold places. The mammals that live on mountains cope with the cold by having an extra-thick coat of fur. They also have specially-shaped feet and toes to help them to move quickly and safely over the rocks. In their mountain home, they are safe from many of the hunting animals that live on lower ground.

Born climbers

Goats eat almost any plant food and they will climb almost anything to get at it. In some places, goat flocks have made the ground almost bare.

Hooves have hard edges, but are rubbery underneath – just like the soles of climbing boots.

Small hooves make it easy for a goat to get a foothold on rocky ground.

Chinchillas eat grasses, and plants that grow near the ground.

Brushlike tail

Thick, dense fur is a blue-gray color.

Rock hyraxes feed on the grass of the African plains.

Well wrapped up

The Andes Mountains of South America are home to the chinchilla – a mountain mammal with a luxurious fur coat. At one time, wild chinchillas were very common. Today, they are rare, because too many have been hunted for their valuable fur.

Mountains in the grass

In some parts of Africa, giant boulders are piled together in heaps above the grassy plains. These small-scale mountains are the home of hyraxes. A hyrax is about as big as a rabbit.

Rock hyraxes sweat with their feet. The sweat forms a sticky layer that helps the hyrax grip the rock surface.

Desert mammals

During the day, it's hard to spot any animals in a desert. The sun's heat is fierce, so desert animals hide away in the shade. But as soon as the sun sets, things change. Mammals wake up from their daytime sleep and leave their hiding places to look for food. In the darkness, the desert comes alive.

Seed collectors

When night falls, these pallid gerbils come out to collect damp, dewy seeds. They bring them back to their burrow, where the atmosphere makes the seeds even damper. This way, the gerbils get enough water to keep them going.

Gold color blends in well with sandy habitat where gerbils live.

One hump or two?

A camel's hump is a built-in store – not for water, but for food. Dromedary camels, which live in Africa and Asia, have just one hump. Bactrian camels, from central Asia, have two. Bactrians live in deserts where the winter can be very cold. Every year, they grow a long winter coat.

Camels have long eyelashes which keep the sand out of their eyes.

The mole's thick fur slants backward to keep out the sand.

Sand swimmer

In the desert of Southern Africa, the golden mole "swims" through the sand with its powerful front legs. To find food, it tunnels just beneath the surface. If it senses a small animal above, it drags it underground and eats it.

The golden mole's front paws have strong claws for digging.

Water from food

Some desert animals never drink water. Instead, they get water from their food. See for yourself how much water is in plants. Pick some grass and weigh it. Now put it in a warm (not hot) oven until it turns crisp. If you weigh the grass again, it will be lighter, because it will have lost most of its water.

Kitchen scales and notepad for recording weight of grass

Ask an adult to heat the oven up for you.

Night shift

Coyotes (*coy-oh-tees*) live in North America. They manage to survive in many different places, from deserts and grassland to forests and mountains. Desert coyotes spend most of the day asleep. When the sun sets and the air becomes cooler, they wake up and set off to hunt. Listen for coyotes howling in the night.

Freshwater mammals

Next time you walk along a riverbank, keep your ears open for a sudden splashing sound – this is the noise made by a water vole as it jumps into the river and paddles away. For freshwater mammals such as the vole, streams and rivers are places to feed and also places to hide.

Water slide

Otter families use a muddy riverbank as a fun slide. They tuck up their paws and slide into the water on their chests.

Stiff whiskers feel around in muddy water.

Dinner dive

The otter is an expert diver. It can stay underwater, while catching fish, for as long as four minutes. When it leaves the water, the otter settles down to eat on the bank, holding its prey in its front paws. Look for fish scales and bones by the water – an otter may have just finished a meal.

A tasty meal

Water voles live on plant food. If you know a place where water voles live, try leaving some sliced apple near the water's edge. As long as the voles cannot tell you are nearby, they will come out of the water to feed.

Powerful teeth gnaw through small trees

Beaver builders

Beavers are the engineers of the mammal world. They dam (stop) flowing water with branches and small trees. Then they build a home from sticks in the still water behind the dam. The only way to get to it is underwater.

Powerful tail slaps against the water to warn of danger

Poisonous paddler

Water shrews are tiny mammals that live in streams. You might see one hauling a frog or fish out of the water. They have poisonous saliva that stuns prey, making it easier for the tiny mammal to cope with a large meal.

Hairy fringe on hind toes helps the shrew paddle

When the water shrew dives, its fur traps a layer of air. This makes it look silvery.

55

Mammals of the sea

What is the difference between a shark and a dolphin? The answer is that a shark is a fish, but a dolphin is a mammal. Many other kinds of mammals live in the sea, including whales, walruses, seals, and sealions. And although they look different from the ones that live on land, all these mammals breathe air and raise their young on milk.

Land or sea?
Unlike whales and dolphins, seals and sea lions can move around on land. They hunt at sea, but they come ashore to rest and raise their young. Look out for sea lions like this one sunbathing on rocks by the sea.

Making music
Dolphins are sociable animals – they communicate with each other by whistling, clicking, and even singing. They also use some of these sounds to find food.

Back flippers can point forward to help sea lion move on land

Bones on the beach

If you go beachcombing after a storm, look out for bones that have been thrown up by the waves. You may find a seal or sea lion skull – the teeth are sharp and look like dog teeth.

Seal skull with sharp front teeth

Whale watching

In some parts of the world, you can watch whales as they swim close to the shore. A killer whale's black and white markings and big fin make it easy to recognize.

Look for a large fin shaped like a triangle.

Up to 50 whales hunt together in a pack called a pod.

Whales often trap schools of fish in a cove.

Careful killers

Killer whales hunt in packs. They feed on fish, penguins, and seals. Despite their great size and fearsome teeth, killer whales have never been known to attack humans.

57

City mammals

When humans go to bed and a city settles down for the night, a secret band of animals is on the move. Mice and rats scuttle silently over our leftovers and help themselves to a meal. Foxes and raccoons clamber onto garbage cans, and hedgehogs make their nightly patrols for insects and other small animals. By the time we wake up, all these animals are once more hidden away.

Rats will eat almost any kind of food, and they are quick to find ways to get at it.

Unwelcome visitors

Rats are intelligent and inquisitive animals, and a rat can make an interesting pet if you look after it properly. But wild rats are a different matter, because they often carry diseases. At times in the past, diseases spread by rats have killed millions of people.

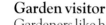

Sorting through the rubbish
In North America, raccoons have been quick to take to city life. They are good climbers and they can run along the tops of walls or squeeze through pipes.

A raccoon uses its front paws to search through rubbish for food.

Garden visitor
Gardeners like hedgehogs because they eat slugs (which damage plants). You can encourage a hedgehog to visit your garden by putting out cat food or bread soaked in milk. Don't put out too much, or you may attract cats or rats as well.

City fox
In some parts of Europe, red foxes are just as much at home in cities as they are in the countryside. Like raccoons, foxes raid garbage cans for leftover food. People who see city foxes often mistake them for dogs.

Night watch
Bright light often scares animals away, so an ordinary flashlight is not very good for watching mammals after dark. Dim red light is better. To make a spotter's flashlight, tape some clear red plastic film over the face of a flashlight.

59

Index

A

apes, 19
antlers, 29

B

badger, 49
bank vole, 25, 49
bats, 8, 10, 22-23, 38;
    Daubenton's, 23
beaver, 55
birth, 10, 11
bloodhound, 14
blue whale, 11

Gibbon

C

camels, 20, 52
camouflage, 42, 43
carnivores, 24
cats, 12, 13, 21, 42;
    defense, 44;
    grooming, 27;
    hunting, 13, 39;
    kittens, 34, 35, 36;
    paws, 20
chimpanzees, 26, 35
chinchilla, 50
cows, 13, 24
coyotes, 53

DE

deer, 21, 29, 43, 49;
    red, 29
defenses, 44-45

Elephant family

dogs, 11, 12, 14, 15, 17, 21;
    grooming, 27;
    movement, 11;
    panting, 17;
    paws, 20;
    puppies, 36;
    senses, 14, 15
dolphin, 11, 56
dormouse, 46, 47

echidna, 11
elephants, 10, 26, 34, 35, 41

F

feeding, 24-25, 41
fox, fennec, 15;
    red, 59

G

gerbils, 12, 52
gibbons, 36, 37
giraffes, 11, 28
goats, 51;
    mountain, 51
gorillas, 35
grooming, 26, 41
growth, 30
guinea pig, 30, 31

H

habitat, 9
hair, 8, 10, 11, 16-17, 28,
    45, 49
hamster, 47
hare, 15, 43
harvest mouse, 30
hedgehogs, 11, 35, 59
herbivores, 24
hibernation, 46-47
hippos, 26, 29
hooves, 12, 20, 21, 51
horse, 12, 17, 19, 21
humans, 11, 14, 16, 30, 34,
    35, 36
hunting, 13, 25, 38-39, 42,
    56
hyraxes, 51

Hedgehog

KL

kangaroos, 10, 18, 19
koala, 48

lions, 25, 38-39

M

marsupials, 32-33, 48
mice, 8, 58
milk, 8, 10, 30, 31, 32, 34,
    56
mole, golden, 53
monkeys, 10, 19
mouse, 20
movement, 11
moving, 18, 20
muscles, 17, 19, 36, 37

NOP

nests, 30, 40, 46

omnivores, 24
opossum, Virginia, 33, 45
otters, 54

pigs, 13, 34, 35
porcupine, 45
predators, 41

R

rabbit, 40-41, 49
raccoons, 8, 58, 59
rams, bighorn, 28
rats, 15, 20, 30, 31, 58
reindeer, 21

Fox cubs at play

S

sea lions, 56, 57
seals, 56, 57
senses, 8, 9, 14-15, 38, 53
sheep, 13, 16, 49
shrews, 38, 55
skunk, 45
sloths, 43
smell, 9, 14, 38
squirrel, 8-9, 18-19, 47
sweat, 17

TV

territories, 28-29
tigers, 10, 38, 42

voles, 8, 25, 49, 54

On safari

W

wallaby, 32
walruses, 56
water shrew, 55
water vole, 54
weasel, 48
whales, 10, 56, 57
whiskers, 8, 15, 38, 54
wolves, 38
wood mouse, 25, 48
wool, 13, 16, 49

Z

zebras, 38, 41

Brown rat

Acknowledgments

Dorling Kindersley would like to thank:
Susan Downing, Sharon Grant, Chris Legee, and Wilfrid Wood for design assistance.
Neil Fletcher for special photography on pages 54-55.
Frank Greenaway for special photography on pages 22, 23, 49, 53.
Tim Shepard at Oxford Scientific Films for special photography on pages 38-39, 46-47.
Michele Lynch for editorial assistance and research.
Jane Parker for the index.
All at Kentish Town City Farm for providing animals for photography.

Illustrations by:
Julie Anderson, Ann George-Marsh, Sophie Grillet, Nick Hewetson, Gill Tomblin, Peter Visscher.

Picture credits
t=top b=bottom c=center
l=left r=right
Steve Gorton: 9tr, 20-21.
Bill Ling: 34-35.
Jerry Young: 14c.
Bruce Coleman Ltd: 59tl; /P. Evans 11cr; /Eckart Pott 48tr; /Andrew Purcell 43br; / Hans Reinhard 29t, 56c.